Scissored Moon

Scissored Moon

Poems

Stacy R. Nigliazzo

Press 53
Winston-Salem

Press 53, LLC
PO Box 30314
Winston-Salem, NC 27130

First Edition

A Tom Lombardo Poetry Selection

Copyright © 2013 by Stacy R. Nigliazzo

All rights reserved, including the right of reproduction in
whole or in part in any form except in the case of brief quotations embodied
in critical articles or reviews. For permission, contact author at
editor@Press53.com, or at the address above.

Cover design by Kevin Morgan Watson

Cover art, "Obsidian" Copyright © 2013
by Jun Yamaguchi, used by permission of the artist.

Author photo by Ashley Elizabeth Photography, Houston, Texas.

Printed on acid-free paper
ISBN 978-1-935708-88-9

For my mother, Sharon Nigliazzo Alexander,
whose illness and death inspired me to become a nurse.

Acknowledgments

The poet wishes to thank the editors of the following journals who published the following poems:

American Journal of Nursing: "In My First Year," "Purgatory," "Sketch"
Annals of Internal Medicine: "Edna"
Bellevue Literary Review: "Divination," "Family Waiting Room," "Relic"
Blood and Thunder, Musings on the Art of Medicine: "Providence," "Transfiguration," "Repose"
The Cancer Poetry Project 2: "Witness"
Cell 2 Soul: "Scratch," "Moirai," "Parlay"
Chest Journal: "Peri-Operative Suite"
Creative Nursing: "Confidant"
The Examined Life Journal: "Metastasis," "Thirty One Minutes"
Harmony Magazine: "Bare," "Manic"
The Healing Muse: "Gush"
Hektoen International Humanities Journal: "Birth," "Greensleeves," "Groundswell," "Proud Flesh"
Hippocrates Prize for Poetry and Medicine 2010 (top entries): "My mother once told me"
Journal of Aging, Humanities & the Arts: "Essential Elements"
Journal of the American Medical Association: "Practice"
Journal of Medical Humanities: "Clean"
Medical Humanities Journal: "Memory," "Sodden"
Pulse Magazine: "Chirality," "Palliative Care"
Pulse, Voices from the Heart of Medicine; More Voices: "Chirality"
San Pedro River Review: "In Situ," "Valediction"
Soapnotes/Third Space Magazine: "Aubade," "Labor," "Cholecystectomy/Rotation," "Source"
Yale Journal for Humanities in Medicine: "Cholecystectomy/Rotation," "What We Couldn't Treat"

Sincere appreciation to Judy Schaefer, without whom this book would never have been possible.

Endless gratitude to Chris, Lola, and Swoopes for their patience and love.

Scissored Moon

Introduction by Tom Lombardo   xi
Foreword by Judy Schaefer, R.N., M.A.   xiii

I

Chirality	3
Rotation	4
Industry vs. Inferiority	6
My mother once told me	7
Source	9
Confidant	10
Bare	11
Clean	12
Transfiguration	14
Sketch	15
Shelter	16
Greensleeves	17
Peri-Operative Suite	18
Memory	19
Malignancy	20
Sodden	21
Parlay	22
In Situ	25
Divination	26
Lesion	27
Metastasis	28
Small Cell Carcinoma Invades the Pelvis	29

II

What We Couldn't Treat	33
Viaticum	34
Relic	36
Labor	37
Pediatric ICU	38
Repose	39

Practice	41
Privation	42
She needs a line	43
Family Waiting Room	44
Every Bed Must Have a Window	46
The Smell of Burning Matches	47
Gush	48
Proud Flesh	50
Thirty-One Minutes	51
Twiddler's Syndrome	53
Sliver of Pearl, Steely in the Gray Sky	54
Aubade	56
Essential Compounds	57
Surrender	58
Screening Exam	60

III

Witness	65
Moirai	66
Groundswell	67
Valediction	68
Providence	69
Purgatory	70
The Palliation of Pain	71
Sepsis	72
Birth	73
Scratch	74
Cachexia	75
Manic	76
Hemorrhage	77
Immortality	78
I paint a book of flesh	79
Edna	80
Sight	81
Palliative Care	82
Epilogue	83
In my first year	84

Notes	87

Introduction
by Tom Lombardo, Poetry Series Editor

Stacy Nigliazzo is an extraordinary combination of poet and nurse. In this debut collection, she joins and extends the tradition of poets who have worked as medical professionals—the physicians William Carlos Williams, John Stone, Rafael Campo and nurses Cortney Davis, Veneta Masson, Theodore Deppe—into her world as an emergency room nurse.

In her poem "Confidant," she wants us to know this:

> I am your nurse…
> No one knows
> the things
> I know.
> …
> Face-to-face
> *I will listen.*

What she hears and sees and smells and touches and tastes is her muse. She collects her figurations from her patients

> like clover
> in the green fleck of my eye—
> like bone chips at the altar.

She builds their sacred images into a sanctuary of the senses, where she comforts their *shivering skin* and catches their *falling tears like rain on wrinkled paper*. She assures them they will not be alone when she hears their *pupils quivering / fighting fruitlessly to stay intact*, that she will be there for them at the end with *my fingertip whispering / through [their] hair*.

At the end of her 12-hour shifts, it's what she can't wash away that we receive: *black clots like a stem of grapes*, or *the woman / wilting // on the pillow of her steering wheel*, or the young woman whose

> … chief complaint
> is pain
>
> from her course red lines
> etched across her forearms.

xi

Nigliazzo's keen eye for figurations is the foreground for her stunning, moving, and highly authentic poetry, while in the background the poet's own mother is losing her battle with acute myeloid leukemia.

Hospitals are not only places we go to die. Often we go to survive, and Nigliazzo's muse delivers us the *breathless little boy* in extremis, whose breathing life she assists stabilizing, she gathers *my arms around him…face buried / in the spire of my breastbone.*

Or another young boy she treats for conjunctivitis after his mother *tapped his eye three times / with a cat's whisker soaked in goat's milk*. The poet-nurse casually remarks *what a handsome boy* and the mother refuses *to leave / until I touched his face.*

Or the 85-year-old woman going into X-ray wearing *her straw hat / proudly, / a silk rose blooming on the weathered brim…and rope-belted coveralls* who says *hold your horses* while she paints *a perfect pink ribbon across her wind-chapped grin.*

Nigliazzo's images do not easily fade away. Her muse, however, comes with a price that both poet and reader pay.

> Twelve hours streaming from my skin
> Like an open wound in the scrub sink
>
> face to face
> in the soap splattered mirror
>
> only then,
> do I look away.

The metaphors and synesthesia belted to the stories kept me from looking away. These poems will bring readers an unusual and rich literary experience.

Foreword
by Judy Schaefer, R.N., M.A.

Scissored Moon hits the shore like a crashing wave of fresh cool surf and a new writer emerges. Stacy Nigliazzo's words are crisp, clear, stunning, and sometimes shocking. I am glad to be here for this moment.

As nurse-writers, our history is limited and our historical narrative brief. A certain amount of courage is involved.

Courage and voice must be truly fine-tuned when that courage and voice turns to the task of creative writing. In the young nurse we often ask: Does the idealism of young nurses wither and erode over time? What sustains meaning and value for their chosen profession? What sustains them in the 24/7/365 grind? There is nothing unique to the practice of the nursing profession that makes the nurse immune to cynicism—to withering idealism. Poetry "read" and poetry "written" has a healing influence and also sharpens the intuitive sense.

Once out of the format of mundane progress notes and journal articles, nurses tend to be silent.

While the silence is often respectful of their patients, it is often fearful of their administrators.

Those who are not silent, have profound and sometimes shocking things to say. On the other side of silence, nurse-poets particularly because of their condensed and precise language, are creating new voices and new streams of myth. And in doing so, cynicism is reduced and idealism sustained in a lively and everyday kind of way that takes the nurse back to the wards—again and again—to do the job of nursing. Nigliazzo is one of those nurse-poets.

Mythic language
Nursing in today's world is highly intellectual and technological and still a hands-on task oriented profession. Nigliazzo, as intellectual nurse writers before her, knows how to work with myth and with other literary devices. She thereby turns myth into her nursing reality. Myth, as we know, works metaphorically and functionally on a subconscious level of deeply embedded and long held belief in a particular story or parable that has multiple meanings.

A poem in this collection, "Purgatory," alludes to the same myth used by Dante, for instance, and allows the reader to imagine the "hell" of an emergency room as "The waiting room is bleeding/ seething, swelling...". The movement in the poem is riveting as Nigliazzo shares the emergency room's environment with the reader. A later poem titled "Transfiguration" leads us to experience a drug induced seizure with mythic overtones.

Nursing continues to be a highly regarded profession of hands-on caring and real numbers; finite ratios of nurse to patient based on acuity, are recommended for delivery of safe healthcare. In most areas of the globe, nursing professionals are in short supply and issues of mandatory overtime and negative work stress are daily concerns for the working nurse as well as their administrators and educators.

Writers such as Nigliazzo give another side of the story. The writing is healing for the writer no doubt and healing for the reader. Additionally the writing tells a story that the public has not heard in quite this creative way. The nurse's story is especially appealing and often recognized as the other side of the patient's own personal story of illness. The two sides of the story are beautifully written in "Parlay." Our lives go on in parallel worlds—in very different environments—but our lives go on or—they don't!

HISTORY OF THE NURSE-POET

Our history is brief, spanning little more than 20 years. The beginning of creative *Zeitgeistic* writing by nurses was *Visions of War, Dreams of Peace* a collection of creative writing by women in the Vietnam War edited by two nurses, Lynda Van Devanter and Joan A. Furey (New York: Warner Books, 1991). Cortney Davis and I followed with the first international anthology of nurse-only writing in *Between the Heartbeats* (University of Iowa Press, 1995). Our book was followed by Amy Marie Haddad's and Kate H. Brown's, *The Arduous Touch, Women's Voices in Health Care*, including nurses (Purdue University Press, 1999). I was privileged to publish the first biographical/autobiographical anthology about fourteen nurses writing in English, who are prolific poets, *The Poetry of Nursing* (Kent State University Press, 2005). As it turns out we continue to be an eclectic group and the questions remain relative to who we are and into what categories our writing will fall and be judged.

A NEW WRITER EMERGES

Nigliazzo is a new writer whose fresh language splashes ashore. She is emerging quickly and is bringing us full circle within the context of a brief history and a frail humanities framework. Yet this frailty is changing for nursing students, young nurses, and seasoned nurses as the humanities are introduced more and more into the education of nursing students and the practice of working nurses. For instance Cortney Davis's book *The Heart's Truth: Essays on the Art of Nursing* (Kent, Ohio: The Kent State U P, 2009) deserves to be on every nurse educator's shelf right there beside the *Notes on Nursing* by Florence Nightingale (1860). All nurses can read and reflect on the courage of nurses such as Florence Nightingale and Davis and now Nigliazzo, certainly different times and different generations but with a tone that is at once brave, strong, scientific, and resolute.

And in all these previous books, courage is demonstrated and advanced by a strong and vibrant linguistic reference to the pain nurses have witnessed down the years, as Nigliazzo now does in *Scissored Moon*.

Read her poem "Practice" in which she writes "…Angle slightly at thirty five degrees—/pierce swiftly—/advance." She describes her own observations and experiences surely but in so doing, she describes a bigger world of nurses, the nursing profession, medicine, and a healthcare consuming public; she moves the historical narrative of creative writing by nurses into another decade.

I

Chirality

I see myself, always
through a stark looking glass

the fun house view of my own face
reflected in the eyes of my patients—

>   tangled in the bleeding strands
>   that line the gray sclera of the meth addict

>   drowning in the pooling ink that splits
>   the swelling pupil of the hemorrhagic stroke

>   swimming in the antibiotic veil
>   that blurs the newborn's first gaze

My clouded countenance,
ever present—

>   slipping even through parched flesh
>   along the steely glide of the angiocath

>   glistening in the acrid snap
>   of intravenous medication

>   glaring back
>   from the bleach wrung siderail.

Twelve hours streaming from my skin
like an open wound in the scrub sink

face-to-face
in the soap-splattered mirror—

only then,
do I look away

Rotation

for Richard Alford, M.D.

I remember my first day
as a student in the OR. It was winter,

just as cold inside.
We scrubbed

and cloaked ourselves in green gowns.
Shoe covers were required.

Out of the box they looked like pale boats
wrecked

against the concrete floor.
The tread was silent.

        Black blood oozing—

    pink flesh torn away—

the surgeon's blade,
steady across a spider web inside the open abdomen.

    What's this I'm cutting into?

       The omentum, sir.

    How many feet of small bowel in the gut?

       Roughly twenty-five, sir.

    And in the colon?

       Roughly five to ten, sir.

    Hold out your hand—

an orphan with an empty bowl,
complicit without question.

Suddenly slapped within my grasp
—sliding—shapeless—

like a baby bird collected from the sidewalk—
    a freshly incised gallbladder.

It reeked of red earth.
I held it gratefully before surrendering it.

Industry vs. Inferiority

When I was a little girl
I lost my name
and the sound of my own voice—

    buried deep

within the whisper
of my mother's eyelashes,
and the printing of my slippered feet
on shag carpet.

In second grade,
I once earned a prize
for winning *the quiet game*—

    a clear plastic swan
    with blue eyes
    and pink angel wings—

small enough
to fit in my pocket.

My mother once told me

she always wanted to be a nurse
until that night—

volunteering as a student in dress whites,
spreading clean sheets in the emergency department.

Placid silence
severed—

she never knew his name, just that
they were the same age.

She could only think to say
I'm sorry—

trembling hands through matted tresses,
latex fingers thick with rushing clots.

Motor vehicle collision—
blunt force trauma—

family
contacted by the attending physician—

none   came.

She covered him
in starched white, binding mitered corners.

Held his hand
as the chaplain painted his forehead.

      Walked away
quietly, carrying with her

always
the salt of his flesh

and the

          fleeing   o f   his

                                    eyes.

Source

He purged the sick with glinting blades.
Flayed their pain

into a sterile bowl.
Painted snowy trees on his days off

to try to forget.
When the white ran dry

he crushed pills to paste,
rounding out the landscape.

I carry his name,
dark hair and stethoscope;

spin words from thread to silver
on my days off

to try to forget.

Confidant

I am your nurse.

No one knows
the things
I know.

My ears hold sanctuary,
sacred words, kept

from
        fathers
                mothers
                      children
                            husbands
                                    wives.

Chief complaint: sore throat—
white lie.

Quick by the admissions clerk,
swift exam
by the physician.

There was more to the story.

        Confessional gown;
faded blue-green squares—
cotton ties across your naked back.

Shivering skin,
falling tears like rain on wrinkled wax paper.

Face to face—
I will listen.

Bare

He has lost his words—
swallowed them up

inside the plastic tube through which he now breathes—
but still, I hear

     his pupils quivering,
fighting fruitlessly to stay intact—
slowly spilling over like bursting ink wells;

     his fist clenched
mightily around the latched siderail—
refusing to let go;

     his gray flesh howling
Magdalena—whose name is cleaved
against his chest in sprawling red script, bordered with roses.

I reply with my fingertip whispering
through his thick black hair—

quiet flesh
assuring he is not alone.

Clean

Soap and water in the scrub sink
rinsing up to my elbows

Mindful of what remains

What I can't wash away

Black clots like a stem of grapes
against her thighs

A tangle of blood and bed sheets

What she bore beneath split stirrups

Baby boy, slipped too soon
Still and silent

Fingernails in my flesh
as she flooded my arms

The clay of our combined skin

Cradled hands beneath
the white blanket

Tears of my own
when she sang to him

Red container marked "pathology specimen"

Careful not to bump his head
on the jagged, plastic rim

> *A bleeding splinter in my bones*
> *that never breaks free*

Grasping sterile towels
I dry my scoured, shining skin

Reaching for the next patient

Transfiguration

Jane Doe,
adolescent,
        seizure on a city sidewalk.

Rancid flesh—black galls
        painted by the needle in her pocket.

Scrap of breath
        through an empty tube in the ER.

The festering sky
        bleeds gray—

                all that she is and never will be.

Alone, in vain
I weep.

Sketch

I think about the woman
wilting

on the pillow of the steering wheel,
how her blood and breath paint the ground.

Paramedics offer her up
in white splints.

Eyes, brimming black bowls
that can't be filled.

The physician notes the time.

I count the coins in her pocket
and trace with heavy marks her wounds

over buckled lines,
the shape of a woman.

Shelter

He liked to hunt
and to hang his kills on hooks

in the living room.
Lacquered birds, mid-flight.

Head of elk and glass-eyed cat
crouched over the breakfast table.

She flickered
in a spotted robe

like the wing of a buckeye.
He collected her

with snare of fennel
and milkweed,

though she fed
on sand—wreathed a crown

of fine silk.
She grew to love winter,

warm against her pin on the blackened hearth,
wings unhinged beneath wax paper,

fanning embers.

Greensleeves

My breath spins fleeting white,
drawing near the icy blanket of blue flesh

found amongst the sleeting rain
and snow flurries—

uncommon for this time of year.
The quivering fist of her heart

unfurled in faint submission.
I wonder—

who will seek her pressed beneath
stark sheets and warming blankets?

My fingertip tracing the scar that paints
her frigid abdomen—the hallmark

of a child's passage from her body
into its own—

who has loved her?

Peri-Operative Suite

We talk about the incision line, and how the sutures
will cover the butterfly tattoo she hid from her father at fifteen;

and whether *stage three* is considered *late*;

and how the anesthesiologist will help her sleep,
and when the drip stops   how she'll likely come back

     swimming,

hulling the blue air like wheat.

She counted *seven*, back from ten; her skin, the color of rain,

         and the blade guttered.

Memory

Stephanie, age 11, who was brought to the hospital by police after her mother broke a glass serving tray across her foot, tells me about her dream.

I dreamt
I was back at home.

My family was sitting in my
empty
bedroom.

There was an opening
in the ceiling
with helium balloons wedged inside.

A gush of gray water
trickled beneath our chairs.

My little brother and I
crept to the floor, laughing.

My mother turned toward me.

Her mouth and eyes
were missing.

All that remained of her face
was a hollow,
empty hole.

We returned to our chairs.

Malignancy

stage four

She's lost countless coins
and clips;

fishing lures and spoons
to the old magpie.

It gouges

the gaunt scarecrow
with each prize,

disarticulating the limbs and viscera.

Sodden

She trickles
from the waiting room,

spilling over the starched white
of the exam table.

Each movement stirring her skin
like wind-skipped river rock.

She is nineteen years old with a history
of Depression,

two elective abortions,
dental veneers, and breast implants.

Her chief complaint
is pain

from coarse red lines
etched across her forearms—hidden

under lilac sleeves.
        The whole of her,

a quiet stream of rushing water
seeking a vessel

to pour herself inside.

Parlay

> *Acute Myeloid Leukemia.*

Finally,
a reason why she loves to sleep all day

and why there is sometimes
blood in her bathroom—

and perhaps even why she thinks she saw
an angel at the foot of her bed last night.

> *I remember my flight to Las Vegas. It was late and the city lights were blinding, even from fifteen thousand feet.*

Two weeks, her Oncologist replied, when asked
how long, without chemotherapy—

something about *CNS involvement*,
intravenous catheters and a *head shunt*.

> *I tried to play Blackjack, but I wasn't any good. I could never do math in my head.*

A port-a-cath and intrathecal lines were
implanted the next day.

The surgeon offered special clips
so she wouldn't have to shave her head.

> *The showgirls were strikingly beautiful—so much glitter you could barely see their faces.*

It looked like red paint pouring into her veins
when the nurse started the infusion;

she noticed how it stained the bag
and smelled of sour apples and wine.

> *I bought a dress I couldn't really afford,*
> *wore expensive perfume and waterproof lipstick so I would be*
> *perfect—it wouldn't wash off for three days.*

She loved to take long walks on the unit,
pulling her IV pole behind her—

wrote thank-you notes to all who sent flowers,
even though she couldn't have them anymore.

> *It was hard to tell day from night in the casino. There were never any*
> *clocks or windows—just glossy posters and cash machines.*

Suddenly, her face turned gray—like
ashes swept from the fireplace in winter.

Her flesh, a scorching ember
on the blackened hearth.

> *I saw a woman slide two hundred dollars into a slot machine, losing*
> *it all within twenty minutes. She wept inconsolably, right there in the*
> *casino.*

Doctors hovered at her bedside—
slid a hollow tube down her throat

so she could breathe.
Her pulse pled in whispers.

> *At the end of the week, I was stunned to see how much I had*
> *overdrawn my own account.*

She died soon after in the intensive care unit—
two weeks after starting chemotherapy.

> *The flight home was terrifying. We encountered a patch of turbulent air that shook the plane as though it were firing a machine gun.*

Her family collected her belongings
and planted spring flowers at her grave site.

It took her daughter six months
to throw away her toothbrush.

> *There was no one waiting for me at the terminal gate. I hailed a cab and watched as others embraced—*
>
> *wishing I had just stayed home.*

In Situ

He revealed her
diagnosis.

Gave her an appointment card
and a handful of pills.

She took them
home and planted them

in a jar of sand, along
with his words.

Her garden grew lush that final
spring. Failing

by fall. Ash
in winter.

She put away
her seeds and floppy hat.

When the moon shone black she buried
the jar in her backyard,

scraping
the dirt from her fingernails.

Divination

I dressed her wound
after the biopsy,

a scarlet braid
laced with black thread.

She was alone, but spoke of her father at her bedside
attending a bowl of water and sand,

pulling out stars.

He pinned them in her hair and stayed
until I cut the suture.

Lesion

She arrives and he greets her
in a lead shirt.

They enter a room with black
walls and no windows.

She shivers on the table
with instructions not to breathe.

He captures the following images:

>*a gray seed patch,*

>*pea gravel in a fountain,*

>*the face of a split pear.*

When the test is over
he hands her the pictures.

Metastasis

> *And there were ninety and six pomegranates on the sides; all the pomegranates were a hundred upon the network, round about.*
> —Jeremiah 52:23

It came from the lowest
branch, arils steeped

in pulp and wine.
She split

the plucked heart—
weeping thread of scarlet

swaying at her throat—
the needle, piercing

for a necklace.
What she could not prick

she bled
in glass bowls.

What remained, she carved
out

with her fingernail.
She wore it till the skin turned

black, ripping it away.

                Then replanted it.

Small Cell Carcinoma Invades the Pelvis

*The proximal femur (hip) is a common site of fracture
secondary to metastatic bone lesions.*

                1.

Three years since we halved
her left lung citing *clear margins*.

                2.

Three years

since *it came* and clawed the brick
slab—

                3.

curled beneath the kitchen floor
rustling only at night.

                4.

Her breath is full but limbs fail.

                5.

We speak quietly in a dim room,

bow our heads
honoring the sanctuary

of bone—

6.

milk white,
speckled knots of gray.

7.

The femur resembles a snowy birch
on film,

its peak,
a hitch of sky in the pelvis.

What We Couldn't Treat

Her dream of gray owls culling stones.

Black blood in the double-yolked egg.

Three sixes in the key code.

A red chair in the white room.

Her discarded fingernails.

Spent salt meant to blind the devil's eye.

The sparrow on the clothesline.

Leukemia.

Silent crickets at the sick house.

Viaticum

I volunteered to work on Christmas day
because the pay was good.

My first patient had a hemorrhagic stroke
while sitting in a church.

Her family spooned cream gravy over dressing
as she cooed like an infant

wanting to be held,
though I could not carry her.

I administered sedatives
and the doctor slid a tube down her throat

so she could breathe.
Cloaked in lead,

we watched the scanner pour the shadows of her brain
into a bleeding white cistern—

then cold steel and a red balloon
breathed for her.

I tied her wrists to the bed
when she started to hit herself. Gave more

sedatives to keep her
comfortable.

Her eyes congealed like Vaseline on glass.
I brushed her hair

as she died and bowed my head
when the Chaplain prayed.

At the end of my shift I scraped the ice from my windshield
and tried to remember

the last time I sat inside a church.

Relic

Quietly, they concede,
leaving pennies

at your feet.
Clove oil at your bedside.

A constellation of symbols
etched

across the grease board
like cave scrawl.

In your palm, a withered
blade

of split stone. Fluted reeds
like hollow wings in flight.

Eyes closed, lips
unparted,

I collect you like clover
in the green fleck of my eye—

like bone chips at the altar.

Labor

He was her fourth child.
The three before

had been taken by social services.
For the last nine months

she'd worn baggy clothes
to fool the case worker.

We rushed out to the parking lot
with a stretcher and a box of gloves.

The head was out
before we reached the curb.

He was born with a caul—
a veil over his eyes.

She cried and sang *I'll Fly Away*—

       insisted we return it to her pressed to paper,
            unbroken.

Pediatric ICU

> *People have filled the room he lies above.*
> *Their talk, mild variation, chilling theme,*
> *Falls on the child...*
> —James Merrill

When I think of her
the earth is only seed and stone.

A secret door unhinges.

I remember how she cried

and the woman who raised her
forced a dish rag in her throat.

The air is purple and blue—
      the color bleeds

like mulberries.

Repose

for Elsa

She is perfect.

Soft, flowing lips
and summer sweet skin,

satin scalp
brimming with downy black hair—

eight pounds, six ounces.

The Medical Examiner's instructions
are simple:

Bathe and swaddle her, as with any newborn.
Let the parents hold her.

Mother prostrate on a surgical bed—
belly ripe with blood,

arms empty.
Father's flesh is granite.

Late fetal demise, secondary
to placental abruption and cord compression.

There is one
whose arms enfold her—

one who carries her
through the placid waters of the womb

into the bustle of this world,
and beyond.

Gently rocking and cradling—
for this fleeting moment,

more than just her nurse—
her silent shelter,

her sanctuary.

Practice

I cleave the rind
        in twin sagittal sections,

pith and marrow
        spilling through soft white

slit flesh and would-be vasculature
        weeping palpably

within my grasp—
        ripe for the needle

Sixteen-gauge angiocath, intended
        for cases of trauma and severe blood loss—

You should first
        practice on a split orange

Bevel up—

        angle slightly at thirty five degrees—

                      pierce swiftly—

                            advance

Privation

She slept under a scrap quilt
and was so small,

I thought at first she was a child.

She'd slipped from bed
and scraped her knee.

I need a Tetanus shot.

She was 85 years old,
had just declined treatment for metastatic cancer.

Her arm was unspooled thread.

The smallest needle I could find,
5/8 of an inch in length.

I pierced gently, but still
I nicked the bone.

She needs a line,

he says, passing me the tourniquet,
rolling the sleeves of his starched white coat.

Known drug addict and prostitute,
arrested—then observed

swallowing something.
I note the presence of black emesis

in the bedside basin,
along with small white rocks,

seven dollars in change,
two silver fillings and three acrylic fingernails.

Her belly swollen in defiance.
Might be twins this time, she gushes.

*Gunna name them Abraham and Isaac,
just like in the Bible.*

My needle pierces her parched flesh.
The officer winces in disgust.

Can you really see a vessel?

No, I reply, spilling her blood
into brightly colored plastic tubes.

It's not about seeing.

Family Waiting Room

Intensive Care Unit

1. *5 a.m.*

I feel the sharp
sting

of silver thistles in
my hair,

asleep this night
in a hardback

chair cut
from particle board and plastic.

2. *Pancytopenia*

I dream of her fair
skin bled

purple and blue like
blackberries

settled in a cream pot.

3. *Eucharist*

I awake,
teeth pooling, red—then

spit them out—
grasping white shadows

on the cold ceramic floor.

4. *Drape*

The latch, unhitched—
my legs, not

yet awake— riddled with pins,
carry me

through the parting
steel door.

Every Bed Must Have a Window

...what hurts them most is a dark room
—Florence Nightingale

It would be cruel to deny sunlight.
    The absence

of drapery,
    the parched wall.

        Needle of light,

                dust of skin—

dandelion in the widow's pocket.

The Smell of Burning Matches

It came to her from years ago
at a slumber party,

how they wedged a bowl between the panes and bled candles
over rain water, reading the future.

In the radiology suite, *the pictures look the same*, she muses;
how they run like flamed wax.

Afterward, her husband presses. She recounts,
he tapped the screen and mumbled something about rough edges—

like this—

They listen for a storm.
She clears the ledge and trims the spent wick of a clotted candle.

The sky cracks
and the scissored moon cries.

Gush

Emergency triage—calling the next patient.

He rises, a reeling vessel.
Sobbing flesh.
Quicksand anchor.

Walking—
      wading.

Parched and dry, I dive
headlong,
bailing water.

Higher ground—
wrenching the siderail.

Stethoscope on seething skin
leaves an imprint.
Blood and water

paltry sieve.
My ears drowning.
Wailing heart fails.

We breathe
for him. Palm over knuckles
thrash his chest.

Floating veins
leak Epinephrine,
Lasix.

Wall suction,
swift wake, frothy pink—
one liter.

Forty-five minutes—
pen Doppler—no pulse.
Eyes wrung out. Sunk.

Stone white
sheets from chin to foot,
lights dimmed.

Awaiting his wife and daughter.

Proud Flesh

Dank sleeves of fetid gauze
       against her skin,

she arrives in a taxi,
       pre-medicated with Fentanyl.

Doctors say *she is lucky*—

       boiling bath water on a hot plate—
              only her arms engulfed when the kitchen caught fire.

       Silver shears unloose a wellspring—

tears of sanguine flesh,

       blood catkins.

Thirty-One Minutes

1.

My palm enfolds her
mottled chest—sprawling
quiver and swathe—

counting with the clock; compressions
one, two, three…..

2.

Frenzied line, snare
of gray flesh—

less of her now,
three fingertips across her fallow
frame cracking

deeper.

3.

We should stop—can't
stop—sweet sleeping girl,

white ribbons flock her hair,

smaller still—
a solitary petal in my grasp.

4.

I cannot hold her—keep
her—

sullen drop of spring rain
fallen
from my fingernail,

rippling back into the air
before it touches ground.

Twiddler's Syndrome

> *The permanent malfunction of a pacemaker due to the patient's deliberate or subconscious manipulation of the device beneath the chest wall.*

First a tickle, then
a twitch—fiber of a woolen sleeve—

cat's whisker on the cheek at 5 a.m.—
walking cast in summer with the hanger unwound.

It rattles like a box of seeds
beneath the skin,

that tiny square
above his heart flowering wire like ragweed,

keeping perfect time—
tick, tick, tick.

Sliver of Pearl, Steely in the Gray Sky

Wake up spent
at 7:30 p.m. Remember how it feels

to watch the rise and fall of her chest
and match each breath—

to hold her hand
and wash her blood from your bare skin.

Leave your rings on the dresser. Snake
your hair into a ponytail.

Wear her favorite shirt and lavender perfume
beneath your black sweater.

Turn off the radio
and drive into the parking garage.

Take your seat at the bedside.
Open her favorite book and read aloud

the sentences she underlined in red.
Watch how the white pages paint

her paling skin
a deeper gray. Speak quietly.

Pretend you don't know when visiting hours end.
Say thank you

when the nurses bring coffee,
though your throat is granite.

Be surprised at how nine hours can pass like five minutes.
Step out into the courtyard

as the next shift crowds the room
for morning rounds.

Gather green earth in your pocket
and remember that some things still grow,

and will always remain.
Fight with yourself over when to leave.

Take a clean sheet from the linen cart
and wrap yourself in starched white   and breathe

       and wait.

Aubade

> *...take these sunken eyes and learn to see.*
> —Paul McCartney

One of my first patients was a man
with advanced AIDS.

He was admitted with altered mental status
and a fever.

As I leaned over to check his colostomy site,
he smiled and touched my breast,

saying he loved me.

His partner quickly pulled his hand away
and apologized. By this time,

the patient was signing Blackbird
and waving his arms like a symphony conductor.

His partner and I continued the song
until he found

        his moment to be free.

Essential Compounds

Volunteering in my final
winter quarter,

I met her in the Alzheimer's Ward.
Silver tresses swept in braids.

Mother of pearl
eyes

beckoning me to the arts and crafts table.
Not a word—

just her smile,
as I gathered supplies

and worried about my organic chemistry final.
Fretful hands

feverishly constructing mini—molecules
of jellybeans and toothpicks—

Halides
        Alkenes
                Ethers
                        Aldehydes

neatly stacked in candied towers,
high atop a spackled plane.

She watched and waited,
asking suddenly with a spry grin,

    Can we eat those?

Surrender

Breathless little boy. Still
a baby, really.

Neighbors felt him
coughing

through a common wall.
Pulled away

from his mother's bed
by paramedics—

nebulizer stashed
beneath a pile of dirty clothes,

marijuana plants
spilling over his pillow.

Oxygen mask, racemic
smoke, fluttering lines

of pulse and breath on spiraling
white paper.

We prick his vessels,
force

a suction catheter down
his throat.

He does not
resist—

swelling tears on sprawling
white sheets.

Breathing stabilized.
I gather

my arms around him—
flesh bounding

as if to flee his own skin.
Face buried

in the spire of my breastbone.

Screening Exam

1.

It was early.

The street, a slick of black
through severed earth.

The entrance was unmarked.

The winding portal
flanked

the foretelling of a coming remodel—
Pardon our dust.

The clerk filed paperwork and bragged
about a bra sale at the mall.

Five of them, I got, she beamed.

2.

The gown was pink and ill
fitting

like my grandmother's cotton dress that snapped
in front

and hung across her shoulders
like borrowed

skin. Like
bones.

3.

Hold still,
she directed, taping a plastic strip

across my breast,
shaping my arm above my head like a ballerina

as the machine scoured
and hummed—

a twisting vice, graceful against my skin.

4.

This comes off before the ultrasound,
she said,

tearing it away.
I winced and wondered how topless

dancers stand the sting of tassels
once removed.

A slather of green
and we watched the waves that wind

beneath my flesh on a black
and white screen.

Secrets of my body now revealed
to others—to everyone inside this room—

but not to me.

III

Witness

Portal of flesh
perched just above the left breast—

better for chemotherapy
since her veins *like to blow.*

Surgically placed three days prior.

He rifles through the chart, strips away
the spent gauze.

Are you gonna do my head shunt, too? she whispers.
They say it's in the brain now.

He does not reply.

Scribbles a few hurried lines.
Closes the door.

In the mid 14th Century, doctors walked the streets
in waxen coats—observed the masses

from behind a mask shaped like a bird's beak.
Stuffed the tips with flowers and spices

so as not to smell the afflicted.
Wielded wooden sticks to prod away the dying,

lest they be touched.

The window
above her bed overlooks a bustling courtyard.

Blackbirds on the slanted sill
roost in nests of scattered refuse—

whistle elegies and lullabies.

Moirai

I. *Clotho*

Fleck of fiber,
        petal of rain—

sullen fig carried from the womb,
        three days apart—

she cries,

        quietly relents—

                steel and plastic through her vein,

                              thread of hope—

II. *Lachesis*

she wanes—gray
        floret, flamed with fever—

                I flood the dim line,

                        scaling each rale, fluttering heart's breath—

III. *Atropos*

scissors
        deep in my pocket—

                pleading—

                        praying—

Groundswell

Watering green ribbons
illuminated—

my hands across
her gravid flesh

like flowering branches, ripe
against the glaring sun—

Doppler dowsing a fluid path
in search

of a whispering heartbeat.
Her eyes, unraveled—

gathering tears of trepidation
and joy.

      Breathless

           silence—

                suddenly,

                      a ripple of sound—

            slightly muffled at first,

        then resonating,

    soft,

            like spring rain

                spilling

            over a swelling riverbed—

                Fetal heart tones detected,
                Lower left abdominal quadrant:
                167 beats per minute.

Valediction

Whisper of gray
flesh. Ventilator bleeding

plastic air. Sliver of sun
through wooden window slats.

I am the needle—

the weeping blood on bone—
the ripple of pulse and breath

on spiraling wax paper.
I carry you

like butterfly wings, like phantom
threads of milkweed silk

slack against the threshing
floor,

eager for the spinning thatch,
and cloud shift.

Providence

Four months old,
> cradled in the crook of his mother's elbow.

He ain't actin' right.

Plucked from the waiting room,
> pediatric bed.

> Squalling skin—

>> Scampering heart rate—
>>> tiny machine gun belting bullets.

Feeding bottle,
> sappy liquid, dark and sticky.

Is that grape juice?

No.   Mother popping the lid
>> *It's Coke.*

Purgatory

The waiting room is bleeding
    seething, swelling

Spilling into the circle drive

Cigarettes burn the black threads
    of the night sky

Nurse behind the bulletproof glass
    takes the old man first

Spattered scrubs like armor

   Stupid bitch,
     it was my turn

Rage—and sickness—
    gushing horde, gaping

Every stranded soul, her patient

        Her voice, a razored sliver
     calling sanctuary

The Palliation of Pain

from Latin, "palliare" (to cloak)

It is very early or very late.

She plucks a petal from the dim
sky for her empty pocket

trying not to close
her eyes,

focusing on the overhead light
shifting

from a silver-sunned orb
into a blazing copper penny—

                                       my hand, a laden stile
                                            emptying the syringe.

Sepsis

I wanted to hold her hand
and stroke her hair—

wax paper flesh
fired red by fever

blood and bone boiling
in a black well of cancer
    and its cure—

the nurse in white scrubs
said it was okay to

    touch
               her

I gathered a lock of stray hair
from her pillow

and gently
kissed her forehead

writing later in the chapel
wishbook,

    please, God
        give my mother a good death

returning to her bedside
late that evening—

a purple bruise ripe
above her quivering brow—

betraying
my last kiss

Birth

The ubiquitous nature of bacteria,
we hope to demonstrate,

using sterile cotton swabs
and flowing blocks of agar—

      thickly gray and gelatinous,
          poured in rigid plastic plates—

ripe for inoculation.

We tear away each swab's thin sleeve
and slide the soft tips

      over the door handle and the lab desk,
        microscope,

            my fingertip
                and the fluid curve
                    of my climbing collarbone—

then across the prepared media.

    After three days,
we observe the following results:

lush gardens
bursting through the verdant plates—

swelling green and yellow spirals
alive in the viscous soil,

flowering.

Scratch

Together, they find the doorstep.
One cries

and whips her tail
along the icy hinges.

The other plants
a greasy bootprint square

across the parting steel portal,
venturing inside where it's warm,

and there is food—
and people are paid to care about him.

Quick triage
finds no true complaint.

Proffered treatment is fifteen minutes
worth of kindness—

vanilla soap in the scrub sink,
a pre-packaged half-sandwich,

and his nurse's fleeting smile.

Again, he finds the outer threshold.
Tears the corners from his bread,

marking a trail for his eager companion.
Inside,

the nurses raise the setting
on the space heater.

Cachexia

profound state of ill health; malnutrition, wasting

Breakfast was a cracked
plate. An empty bowl.

It's been months, now.

Blood and scans
confirmed—

a winding root of buckthorn
snared the breech.

Silver blades cut out
what was not vital;

      a needle of sky unfurled.

Two liters bled
from her abdomen.

Sixty pounds lost.

They smile and say
she's *never looked better*—

words like salt
she swallows whole.

Manic

Bustling flesh
dangling from the moon's
icy sliver

Swelling stars splintered
through his
free hand

Tiptoe,
skipping across
the apex of the earth

Winding
freefall—

blurring, blinding—

silver

Hemorrhage

Do tears not yet spilled wait in small lakes?
—Pablo Neruda

They gather in a seed pod

                              filled to bursting without pierce

            or in a sodden cloth

     yet to be wrung

              or perhaps inside the green belly

                                  of a buckled leaf

        ripe with surrender—

I held her hand

              until the fluttering line   flattened

          then left quietly.

Immortality

Her skin was a chaff
of stark white.

Death was a winnowing blade
in a gray pea coat.

She lingered,
a grain of rice in his pocket.

I paint a book of flesh

by quill of needle
and salt,

thread
of vessel and bone,

page of quiver
and soft light swept

across the stretcher's
silver cradle.

The lines
        flutter.

Her eyes
              close.

Edna

She wears her straw hat
proudly,

a silk rose blooming on the weathered brim.
Rope-belted coveralls

tucked with eighty-five years in her back pocket.
Called a cab instead of her daughter or the neighbors—

I just tripped on a tomato plant is all,
it's not like it's a stroke or somethin'.

Hands her nurse
three plastic freezer bags—

Use these for the ice pack, she directs,
propping her purple foot

across the siderail.
Time for your x-ray, ma'am.

      Hold your horses, kid, she quips—

pulling out a floral compact,
painting a perfect pink ribbon across her wind-chapped grin.

Sight

Today I cared for a small boy
with conjunctivitis.

Before bringing him to us
his mother tapped his eye three times

with a cat's whisker soaked in goat's milk.
She nodded quietly

as we demonstrated the proper technique
for instilling antibiotic eye drops.

As they rounded the exit door
I casually remarked,

what a handsome boy.

She returned to the front desk and refused to leave
until I touched his face.

Palliative Care

When I cut the stem
I knew it was just a matter of time.

I cleared the sill
and filled a crystal vase.

The petals unfurled.
The smell of summer pierced my skin

for three days.
When the first leaf fell

I added lemon pulp and crushed
an Aspirin,

cut away all that waned—
the shoots were spry

one last day.
I scattered them over green earth.

Flecks of pollen
stained my lips and cheekbones.

Epilogue

I cradled him, saying
breathe, his eyes

across my
shoulder seeing what I could not see.

                        I'm not

                                        ready,   he said—

fingernails in my skin—
a whispering growl—then

silence.

In my first year

studying anatomy and physiology

I was assigned
a large cat swimming in formaldehyde

for dissection.
I named him Lazarus and cried

when I cut into his face, but marveled

at the bones unhinged,
and the pink muscles, and the gray

viscera.
I sliced one kidney in three parts

isolating the cortex, ureter and veins.

I received high marks,
then tucked it safely back inside, lest he be left incomplete.

Notes

Chirality

Chiral: An object that cannot be superimposed upon its mirror image. The most universally recognized example of chirality is the human hand.
—*Merriam-Webster Dictionary*

Sclera: The protective outer layer of the eye; popularly known as the *white of the eye*.

Pupil: The opening in the center of the eye; allows light to enter; may become abnormally large (*blown*) in a person experiencing a hemorrhagic stroke (*brain bleed*).
—*United States National Library of Medicine, National Institutes of Health*

In a newborn baby, serious eye infections may result from exposure to bacteria during passage through the birth canal. As a preventative measure, infants are treated with antibiotic eye ointment in the delivery room.
—*American Academy of Pediatrics*

Rotation

Omentum: A large fold of tissue covering the stomach; stores fat and is thought to protect certain organs from infection; resembles a lacy apron.
—*Taber's Cyclopedic Medical Dictionary*

Industry vs. Inferiority

Erikson's stages of psychosocial development:

Age	*Virtues*	*Psychosocial Crisis*	*Existential Question*
0-2 years	Hope	Trust vs. Mistrust	*Can I trust the world?*

Age	Virtues	Psychosocial Crisis	Existential Question
2-4 years	Will	Autonomy vs. Doubt & Shame	*Is it okay to be me?*
4-5 years	Purpose	Initiative vs. Guilt	*Is it okay for me to do, move and act?*
5-12 years	Competence	Industry vs. Inferiority	*Can I make it in the world?*
13-19 years	Fidelity	Identity vs. Role Confusion	*Who am I? What can I be?*
20-24 years	Love	Intimacy vs. Isolation	*Can I love?*
25-64 years	Care	Generativity vs. Stagnation	*Can I make my life count?*
65-death	Wisdom	Ego Integrity vs. Despair	*Is it okay to have been me?*

—from *Identity and the Life Cycle*, Erik H. Erikson (1959)

My mother once told me

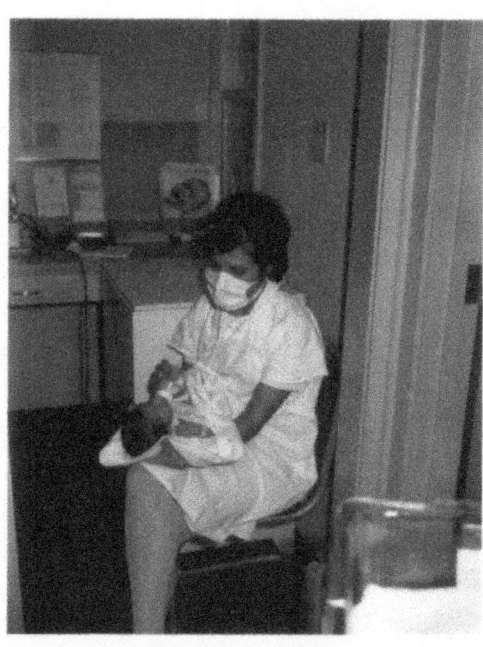

—Sharon Nigliazzo, 1967

Source

—Painting by Luke Nigliazzo, MD, 1965

Confidant

Healthcare Privacy Rule

The *Standards for Privacy of Individually Identifiable Health Information* ("Privacy Rule") establishes, for the first time, a set of national standards for the protection of health related information. The U.S. Department of Health and Human Services issued the Privacy Rule to implement the requirement of the *Health Insurance Portability and Accountability Act of 1996 (HIPPA)*. The Privacy Rule standards address the use and disclosure of individuals' health information, as well as standards for individuals' privacy rights to understand and control how their health information is used. The Office for Civil Rights is responsible for implementing and enforcing the Privacy Rule with respect to voluntary compliance and civil penalties.

A person who knowingly obtains or discloses a person's private health information in violation of this rule faces a minimum fine of $50,000 and up to one-year imprisonment.
   —*United States Department of Health and Human Services*

Sketch

Example of a trauma sketch:

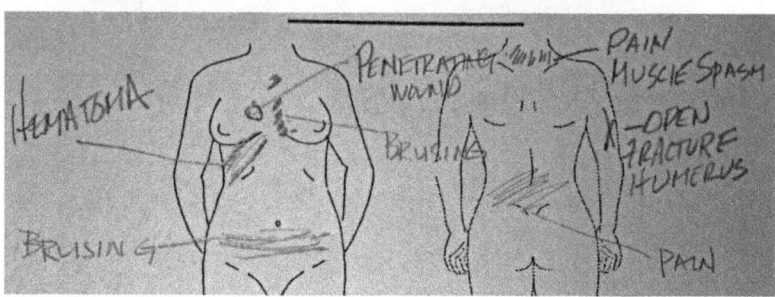

Greensleeves

Hypothermia: (Accidental) A state in which an individual's body temperature is reduced below the normal range (34.4 -37.8 degrees C; 94-100 degrees F). May occur in people exposed to cold weather for prolonged periods of time (i.e., those who are homeless, drug addicts, and alcoholics).

Cesarean birth: Delivery of a fetus by means of incision into the uterus. A horizontal incision through the lower uterine segment is most common; the classic vertical midline incision may be used in times of profound fetal distress.
    —*Taber's Cyclopedic Medical Dictionary*

Lesion

Normal   Cancer

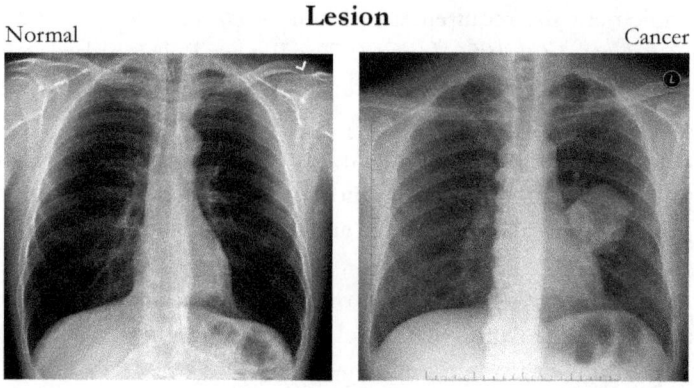

—photos by Dr. Frank Gaillard, *Radiopaedia.org*

Metastasis

How to open and de-seed your pomegranate:

1. Cleave through the crown and pry it open.
2. Fill a bowl with water and submerge the cut pieces.
3. Use your fingers to tear away the membrane; the skin will float to the top.
4. Collect the arils.
5. Be careful where you keep them—they bleed and will stain.

—photo by Elise Bauer, *SimplyRecipes.com*

Small Cell Carcinoma Invades the Pelvis

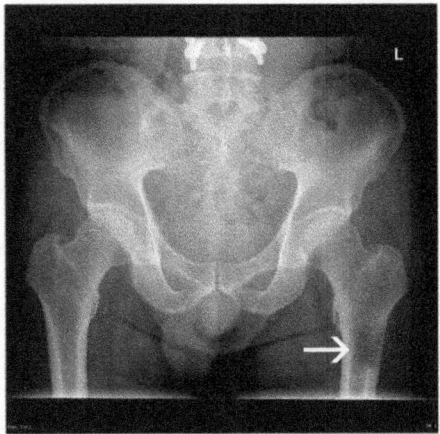

—photo by Dr. Frank Gaillard, *Radiopaedia.org*

Metastases can occur in any bone, but are most often found in bones near the center of the body (i.e., spine, ribs, pelvis, shoulder, skull).
  —*American Cancer Society*

Viaticum

A hemorrhagic stroke (intracerebral hemorrhage, or *brain bleed*) is caused by the bleeding of blood vessels within the brain. As a result, blood clots form and cause severe damage.

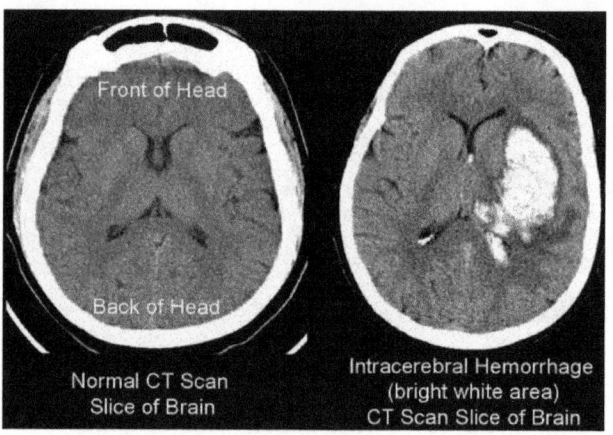

  —*University of Washington School of Medicine*

Labor

Caul: A membrane or portion of the amniotic sac covering the head or face of a baby at birth; rare finding.
  —*Taber's Cyclopedic Medical Dictionary*

Many people believe it is a special blessing to be born with a caul (or "veil"), and that such a child may have divine, intuitive abilities.

Notable people said to have been born with a caul: Edwin Booth, Lord Byron, Charlemagne, Sigmund Freud, Liberace, and Napoleon.
  —*caulbearersunited.webs.com/notablecaulbearersarts.htm*

I was born with a caul, which was advertised for sale, in the newspapers, at the low price of fifteen guineas…
—from *David Copperfield*, Charles Dickens (1850)

Repose

Placenta: A spongy structure in the pregnant uterus from which the developing fetus derives nourishment and oxygen.

Placental abruption: The separation of the placenta from the uterine wall before the baby is delivered; may result in stillbirth from hemorrhage and oxygen deprivation, among other complications.

Cord compression: The obstruction of blood flow from the umbilical cord to the fetus due to pressure from an external object or misalignment of the cord itself; may result in fetal distress if not quickly corrected.
—*Taber's Cyclopedic Medical Dictionary*

Family Waiting Room

Pancytopenia: (*Cell Poverty*) A reduction in all cellular elements of the blood; may cause significant hemorrhage.

Purpura: Bleeding into the skin, mucous membranes and internal organs; initially manifests as dark red or purple, then progresses to blue and brownish-yellow.
—*Taber's Cyclopedic Medical Dictionary*

Every Bed Must Have a Window

Light essential to both health and recovery.

It is the unqualified result of all my experience with the sick, that second only to their need of fresh air is their need of light; that, after a close room, what hurts them most is a dark room. And that it is not only light but direct sun-light they want. I had rather have the power of

carrying my patient about after the sun, according to the aspect of the rooms, if circumstances permit, than let him linger in a room when the sun is off. People think the effect is upon the spirits only. This is by no means the case. The sun is not only a painter but a sculptor. You admit that he does the photograph. Without going into any scientific exposition we must admit that light has quite as real and tangible effects upon the human body. But this is not all. Who has not observed the purifying effect of light, and especially of direct sunlight, upon the air of a room? Here is an observation within everybody's experience. Go into a room where the shutters are always shut (in a sick room or a bedroom there should never be shutters shut), and though the room be uninhabited, though the air has never been polluted by the breathing of human beings, you will observe a close, musty smell of corrupt air, of air unpurified by the effect of the sun's rays. The mustiness of dark rooms and corners, indeed, is proverbial. The cheerfulness of a room, the usefulness of light in treating disease is all-important.
  —from *Notes on Nursing, What it is and What it is Not,*
   Florence Nightingale (1859)

A hospital should provide natural illumination. Each patient room should have a window. If a window cannot be provided, an alternate option is to allow a remote view of an outside window or skylight.
  —*Society of Critical Care Medicine*

> *...Lo! in that house of misery*
> *A lady with a lamp I see*
> *Pass through the glimmering gloom,*
> *And flit from room to room...*
>   —from *Santa Filomena,*
>   Henry Wadsworth Longfellow (1857)

Gush

Congestive Heart Failure: The failure of the heart to maintain adequate circulation of the blood.

Epinephrine: A drug used to treat cardiac arrest; acts quickly to improve breathing, stimulate the heart, and raise blood pressure.

Lasix: A potent diuretic; first-line agent in the treatment of congestive heart failure.

Pulmonary Edema: Possible complication of congestive heart failure; life-threatening; the left ventricle of the heart fails to effectively pump out the blood it receives from the lungs, building pressure in the heart, causing fluid to back up into the lungs. Symptoms include swelling, extreme shortness of breath, chest pain and coughing up bloody, frothy expectorant.
　　　—*Taber's Cyclopedic Medical Dictionary*

Proud Flesh

Fentanyl: An opiate medication used to treat severe pain; approximately 100 times more potent than Morphine; available as a skin patch, lozenge, pill or injection.
　　　—*Taber's Cyclopedic Medical Dictionary*

Twiddler's Syndrome

A pacemaker is a small device that is placed in the chest or abdomen to help control abnormal heart rhythms. This device uses electrical pulses to prompt the heart to beat at a normal rate.
　　　—*United States National Library of Medicine,*
　　　　National Institutes of Health

Essential Compounds

1. Halide: a binary compound of halogen with a more electropositive element or radical.

2. Alkene: any of numerous unsaturated hydrocarbons having one double bond.

3. Ether: any of a class of organic compounds characterized by an oxygen atom attached to two carbon atoms.

4. Aldehyde: an organic compound characterized by a carbonyl group attached to a hydrogen atom.
 —*Merriam-Webster Dictionary*

Moirai

Greek legend tells of three "spinning fates" who would first visit a child on the third day after birth: one to spin the thread of life, another to measure it, and one at the end of life, to cut it.

The fig is a symbol of maternal nourishment and procreation.
 —*The Complete Dictionary of Symbols; Jack Tresidder (2004)*

Early-onset Neonatal Sepsis: A blood infection that occurs during the first week of life; fever (body temperature greater than 100.4 degrees) is often the first sign; late symptoms (such as breathing difficulty, listlessness and erratic heart rate) often do not occur until death is imminent and unpreventable; more common in pre-term infants.
 —*United States National Library of Medicine, National Institutes of Health*

Providence

There are harmful biochemical effects associated with soda intake in children. An average 12-ounce can contains around ten teaspoons of sugar. This sugar isn't partnered with any nutrients to slow down the absorption of sugar (i.e., protein, fiber, or fat), so it enters the bloodstream rapidly, causing a roller coaster effect. Soda also contains caffeine, which is a stimulant. In infants, consumption of caffeine can cause the heart to race and lead to serious arrhythmias.
 —*University of Michigan Health System*

Sepsis

Septicemia: The spread of an infection from its initial site into the bloodstream; can lead to a life-threatening systemic response that compromises blood flow to the vital organs.
    —*Taber's Cyclopedic Medical Dictionary*

Hemorrhage

The Pablo Neruda epigraph is from *The Book of Questions* (Copper Canyon Press, 2001).

Sight

Mal de ojo: Also referred to as *strong eye*; recognized by certain Latin cultures as a type of enchantment in which a person in a position of power can prevent a child from thriving by staring at him with envy or admiration. This may be cured, some believe, by having the person touch or carry the child.
    —from *Curanderos and 'mal de ojo'*
      Silvia Casabianca (2013)

STACY R. NIGLIAZZO is an emergency room nurse. Her poems have appeared in numerous journals including *Journal of the American Medical Association*, *Yale Journal for Humanities in Medicine*, *Third Space* (Harvard Medical School), *American Journal of Nursing*, *Annals of Internal Medicine*, and *Annals of Emergency Medicine*. Her poem "Relic" was a finalist for the 2012 Marica and Jan Vilcek Poetry Prize. She reviews poetry for the *American Journal of Nursing* and the *Bellevue Literary Review*. In addition to her R.N. degree, she holds a B.S. in psychology from Texas A&M and has been recognized by Elsevier for nursing excellence.

Cover artist JUN YAMAGUCHI was born in Japan and still lives there. As a child he loved reading books and drawing pictures but stopped at some point during a period of time he refers to as his "own hell." Later in life, Jun discovered the process of taking photographs and painting using his iPod Touch, using photo processing software from Apple's iOS market. "Obsidian" is one such image created entirely on his iPod Touch that is part of a series of images using the moon as a recurring theme. Jun has no formal training in art or photography and works by intuition.

You can find more of Jun's art at www.flickr.com/photos/monowave and at monowave.jimdo.com.

www.ingramcontent.com/pod-product-compliance
Lightning Source LLC
LaVergne TN
LVHW041339080426
835512LV00006B/541